Coloring book

"A magical world of colors awaits you in our cute animals coloring book".

I would appreciate an opinion on my book

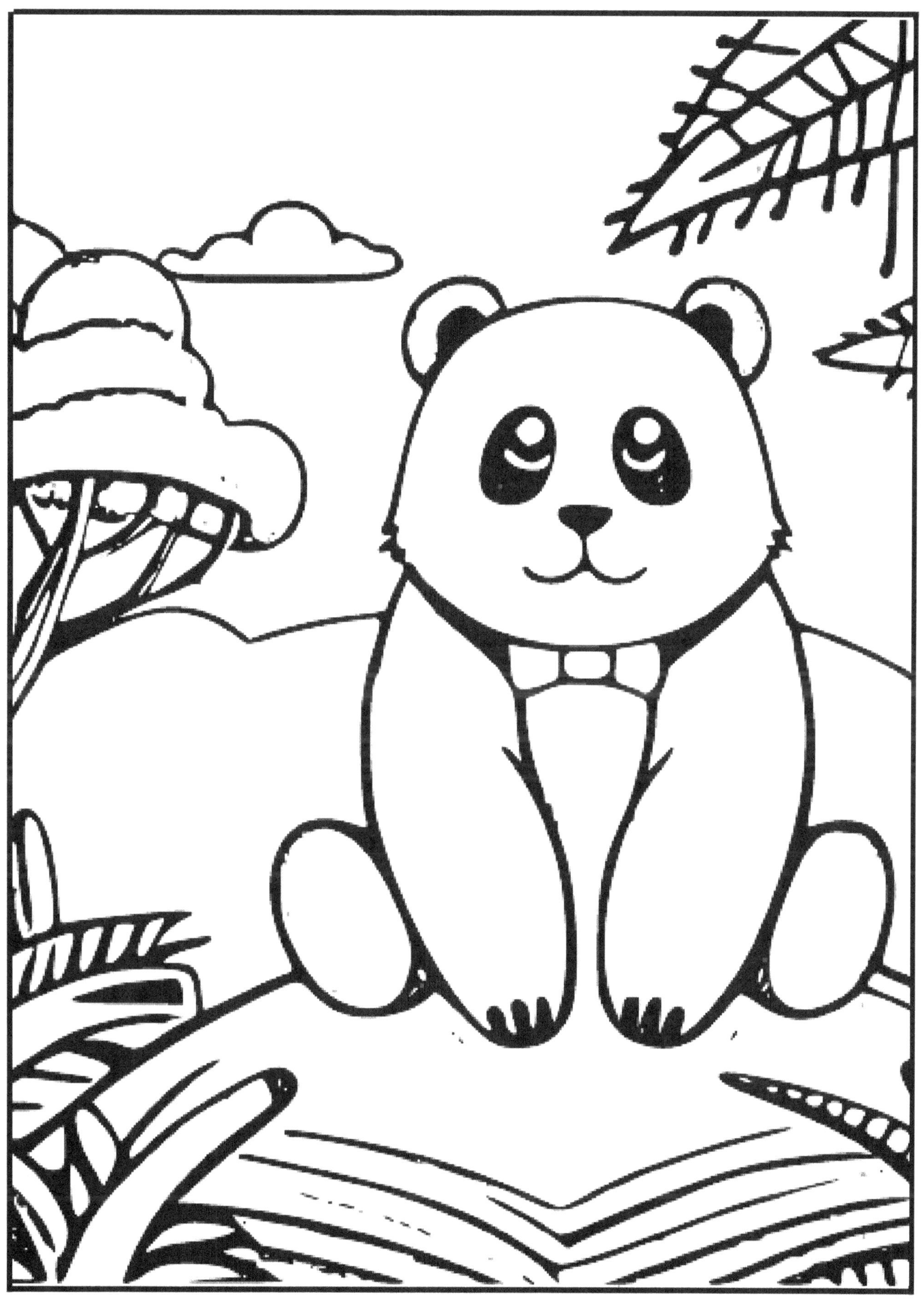

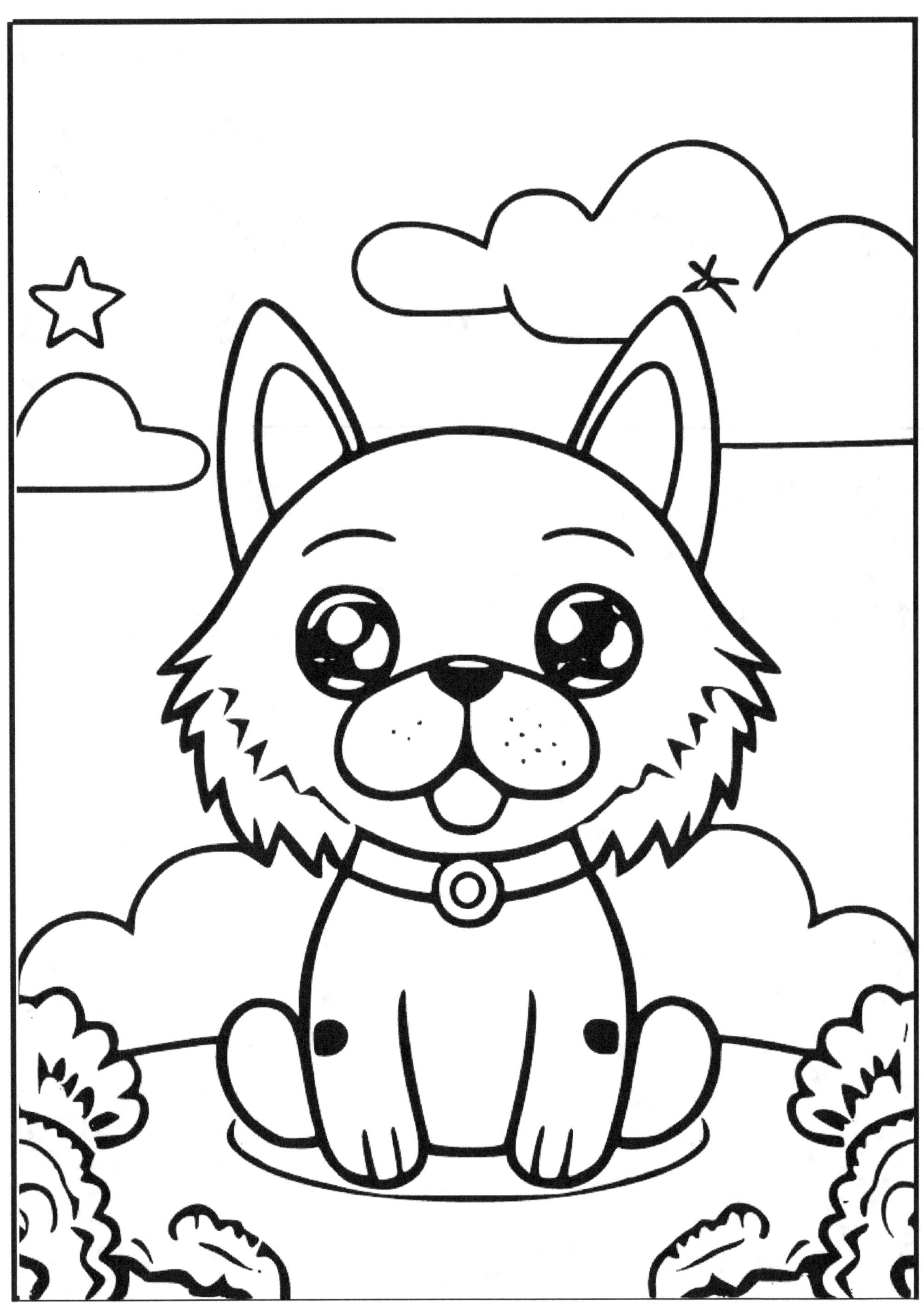

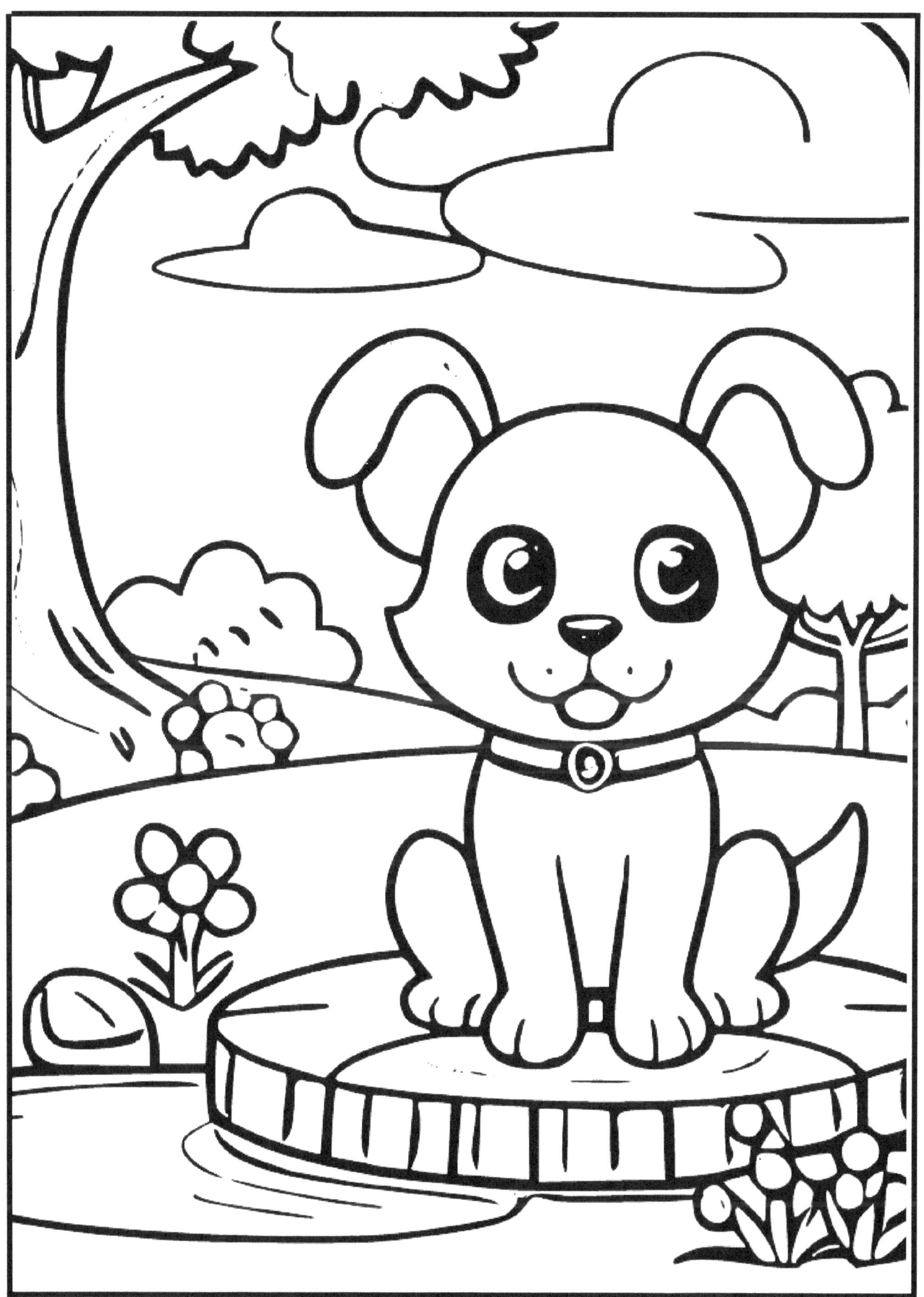

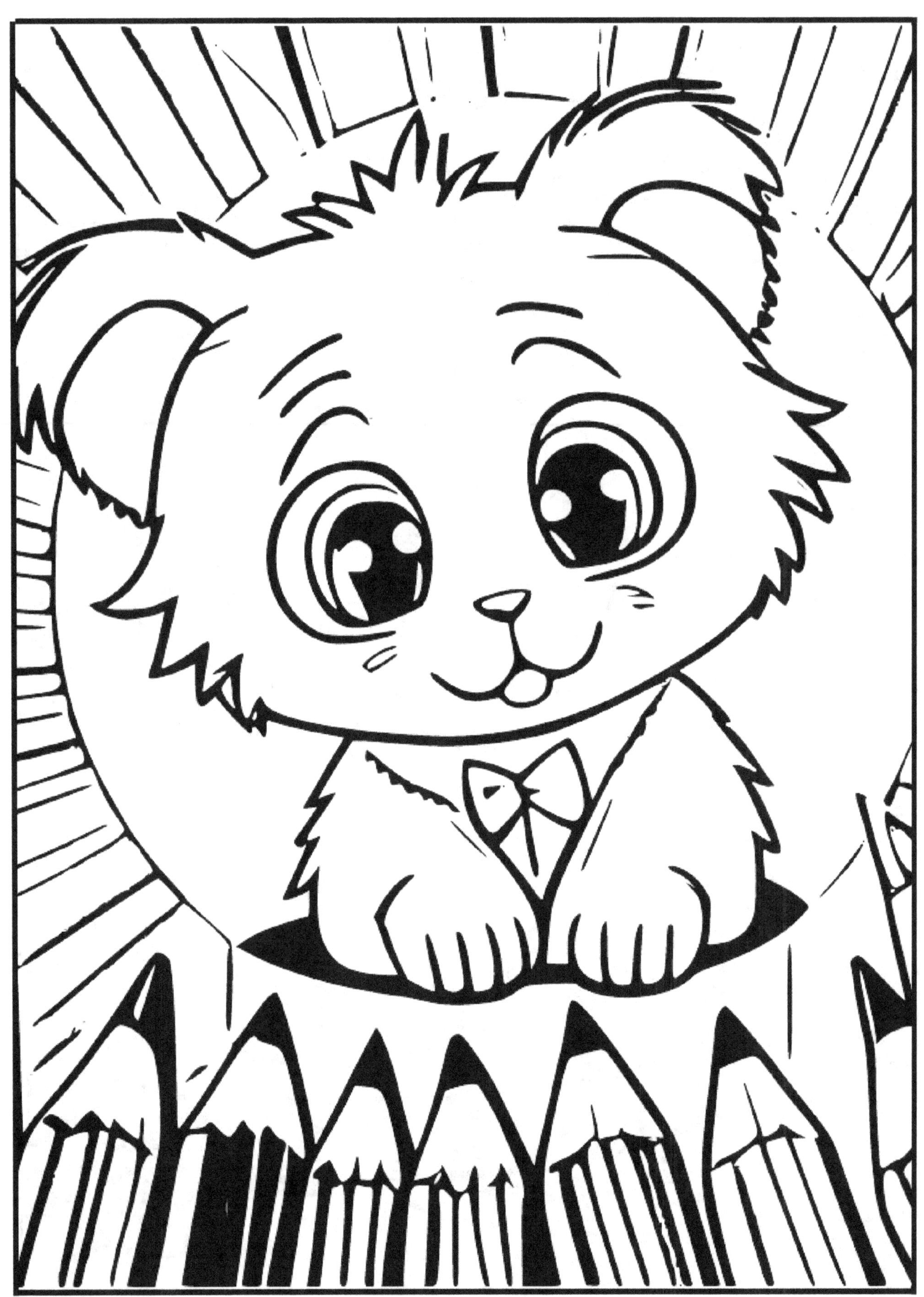

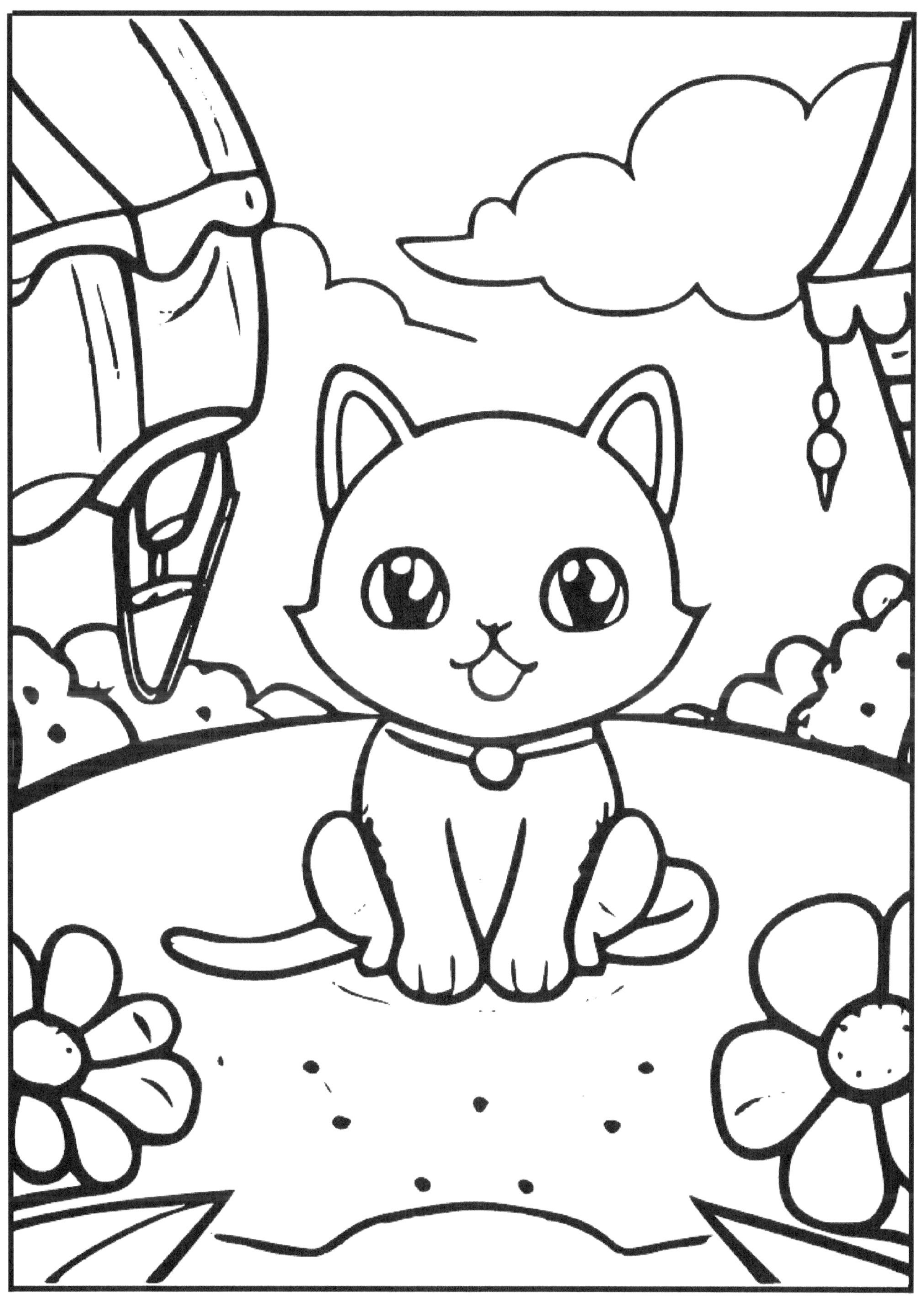

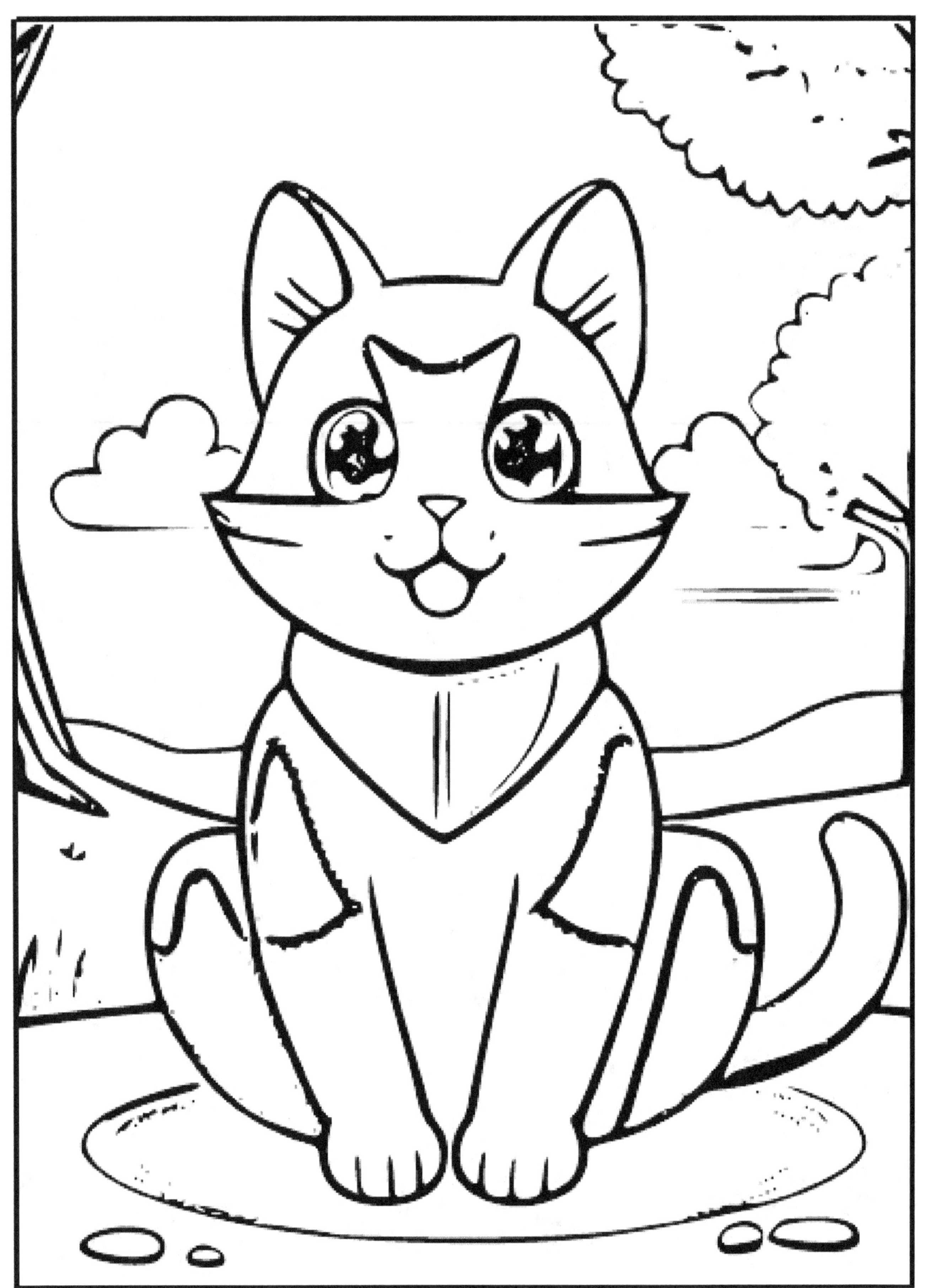

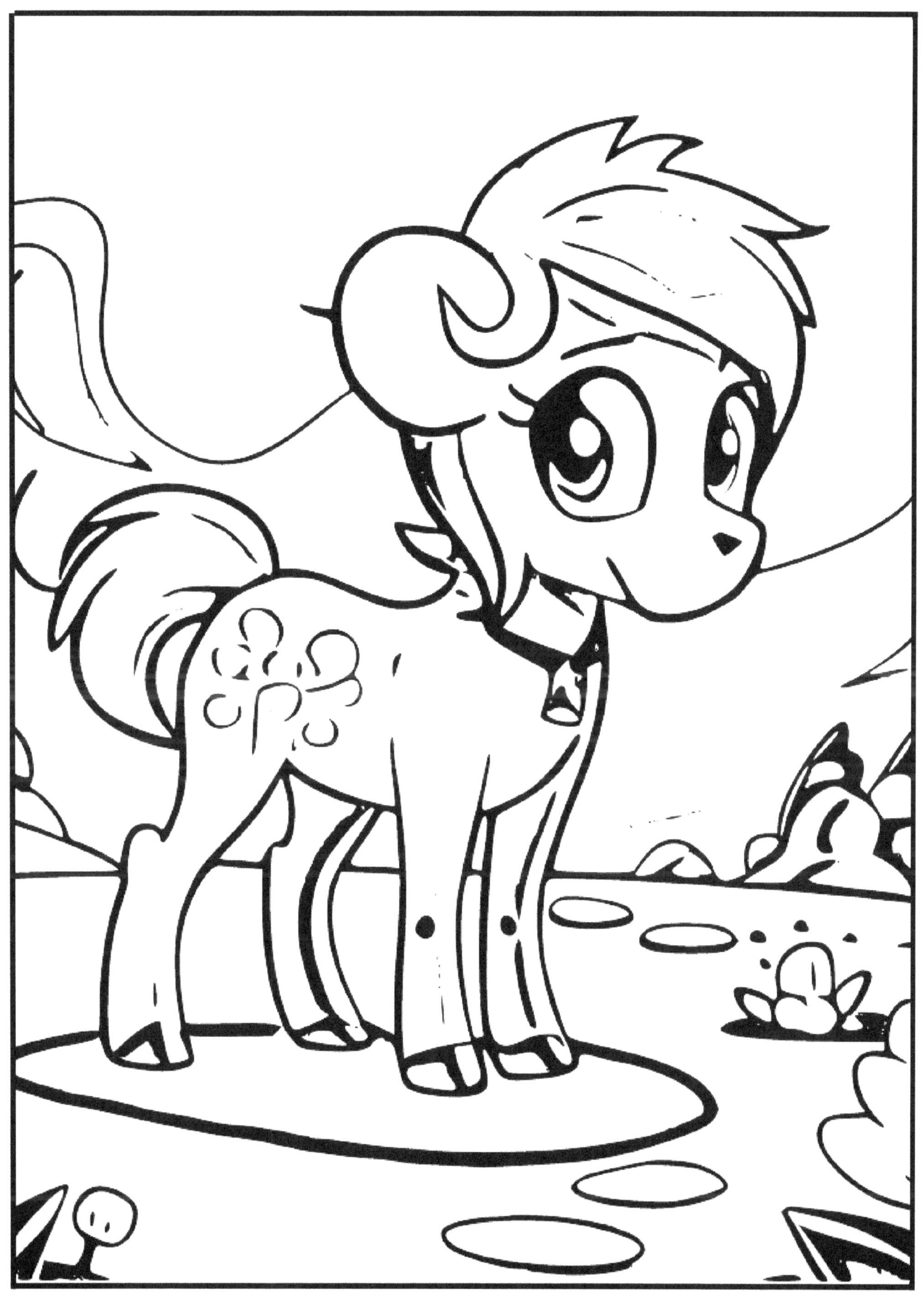

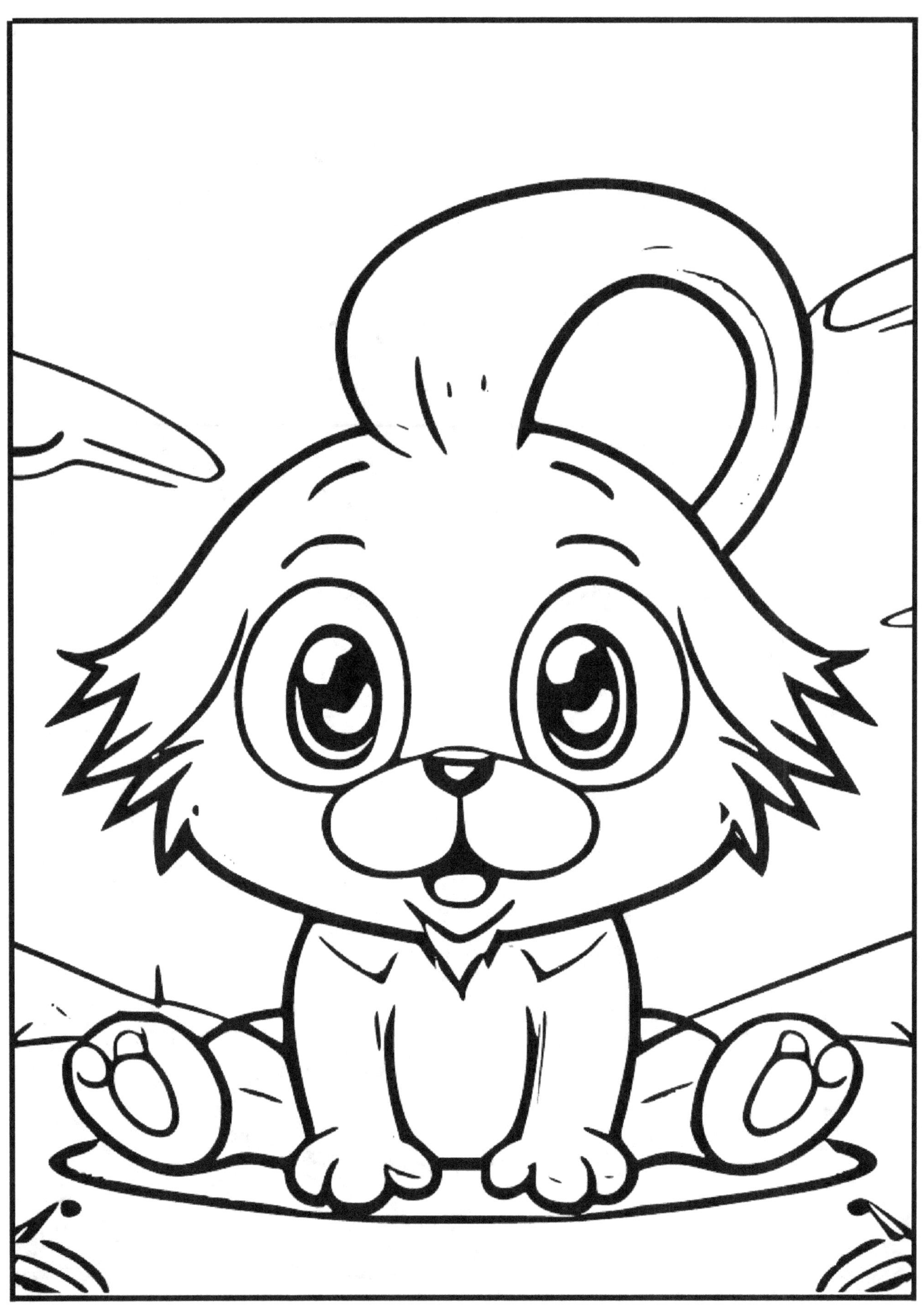

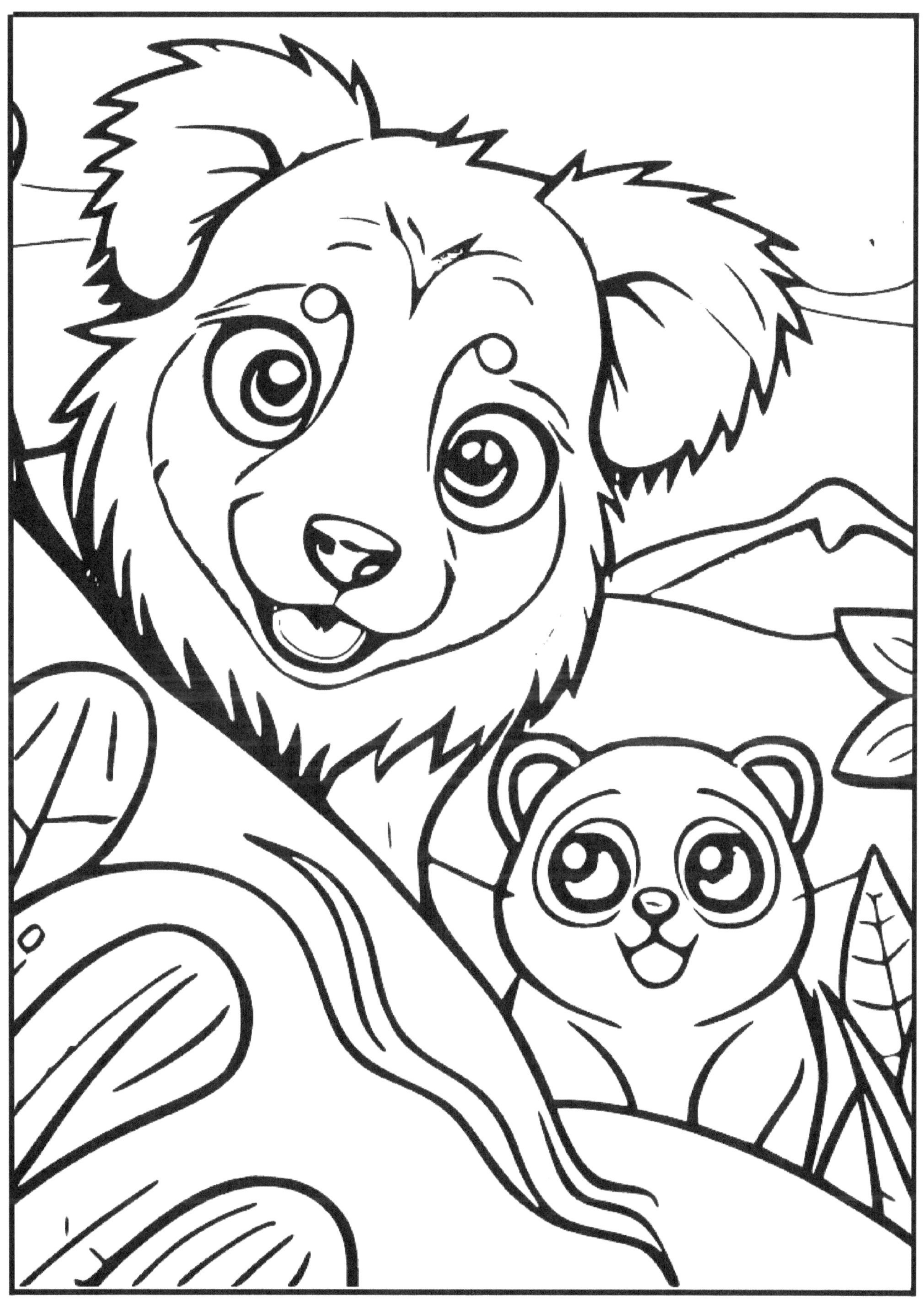

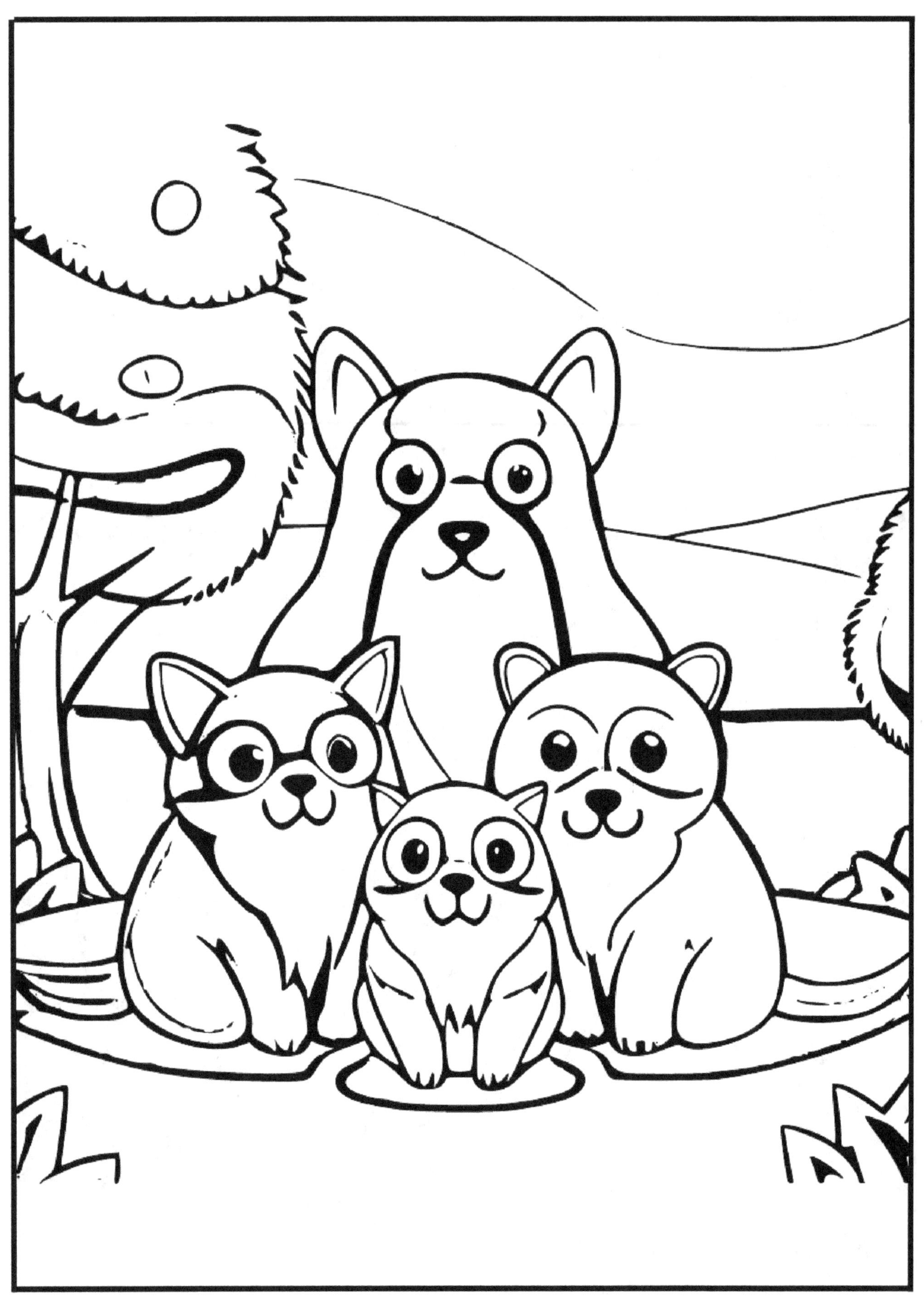

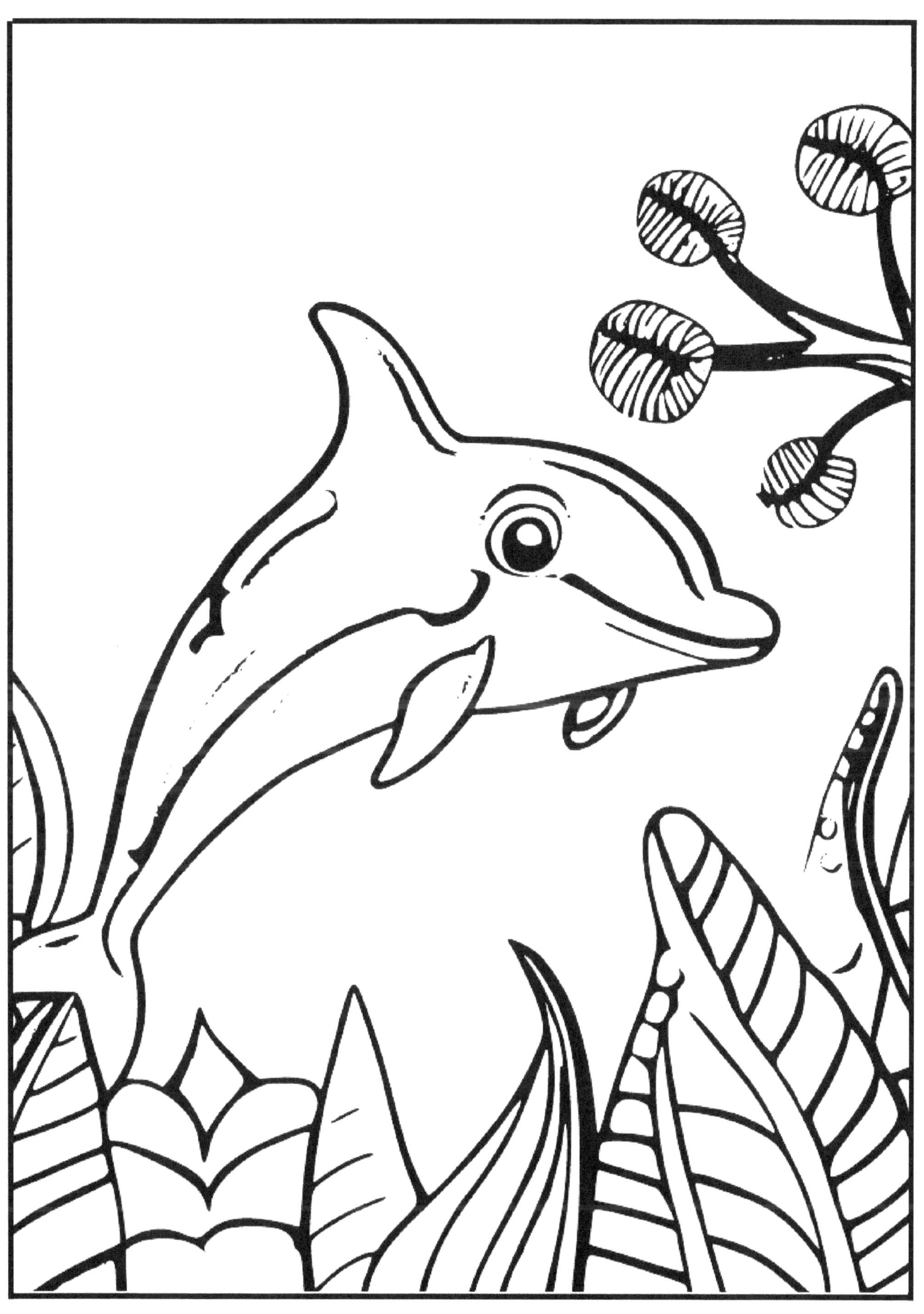

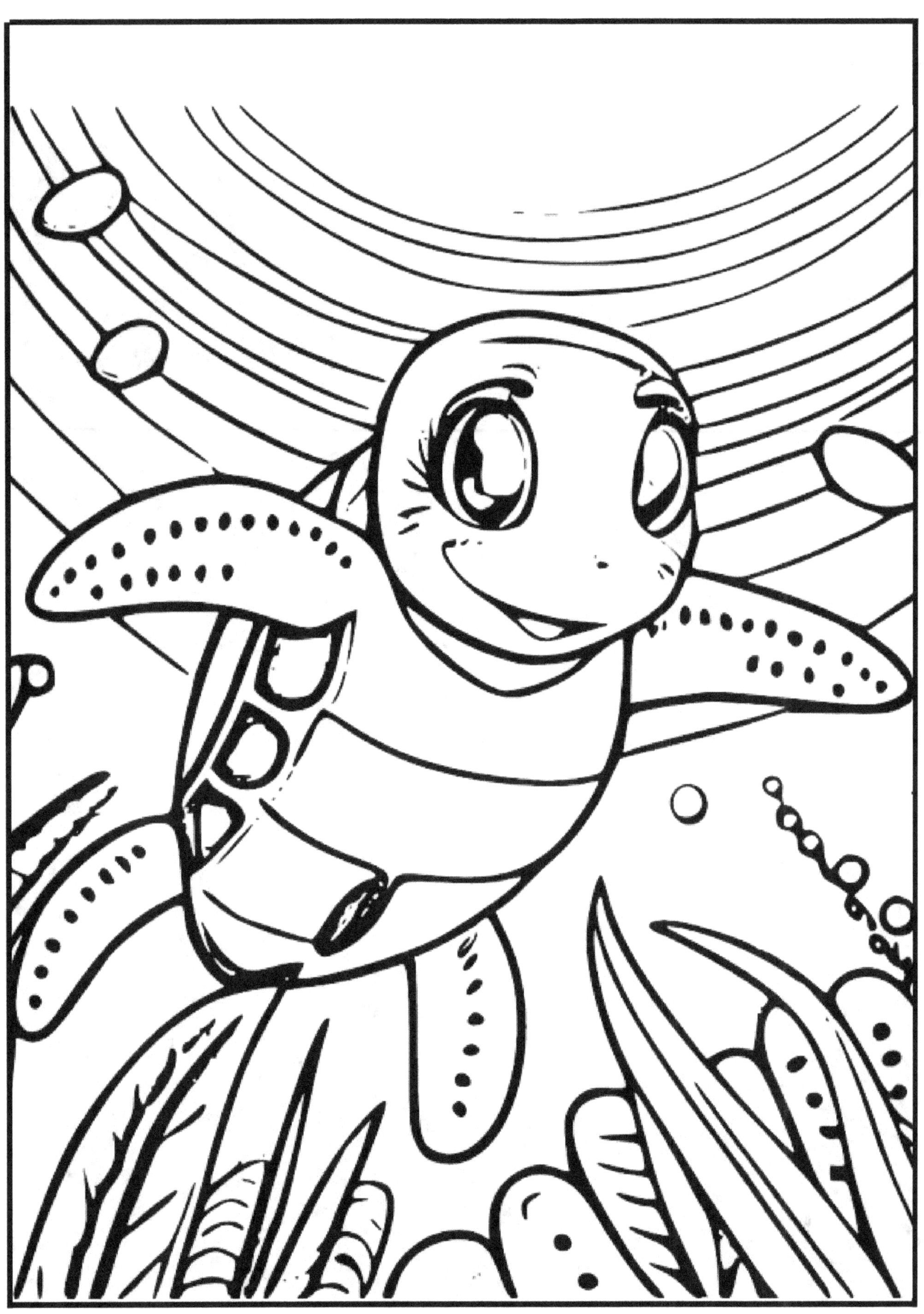

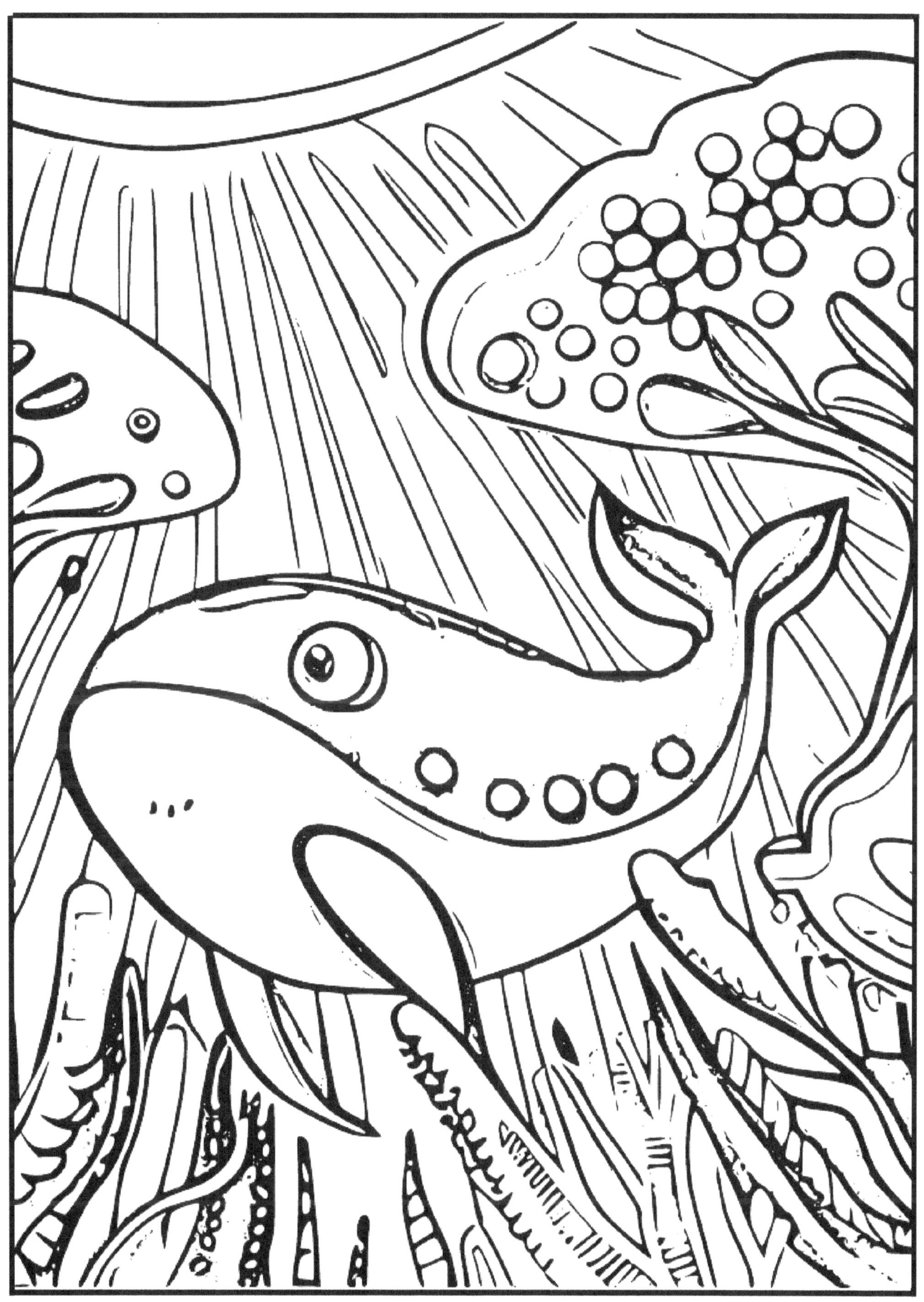

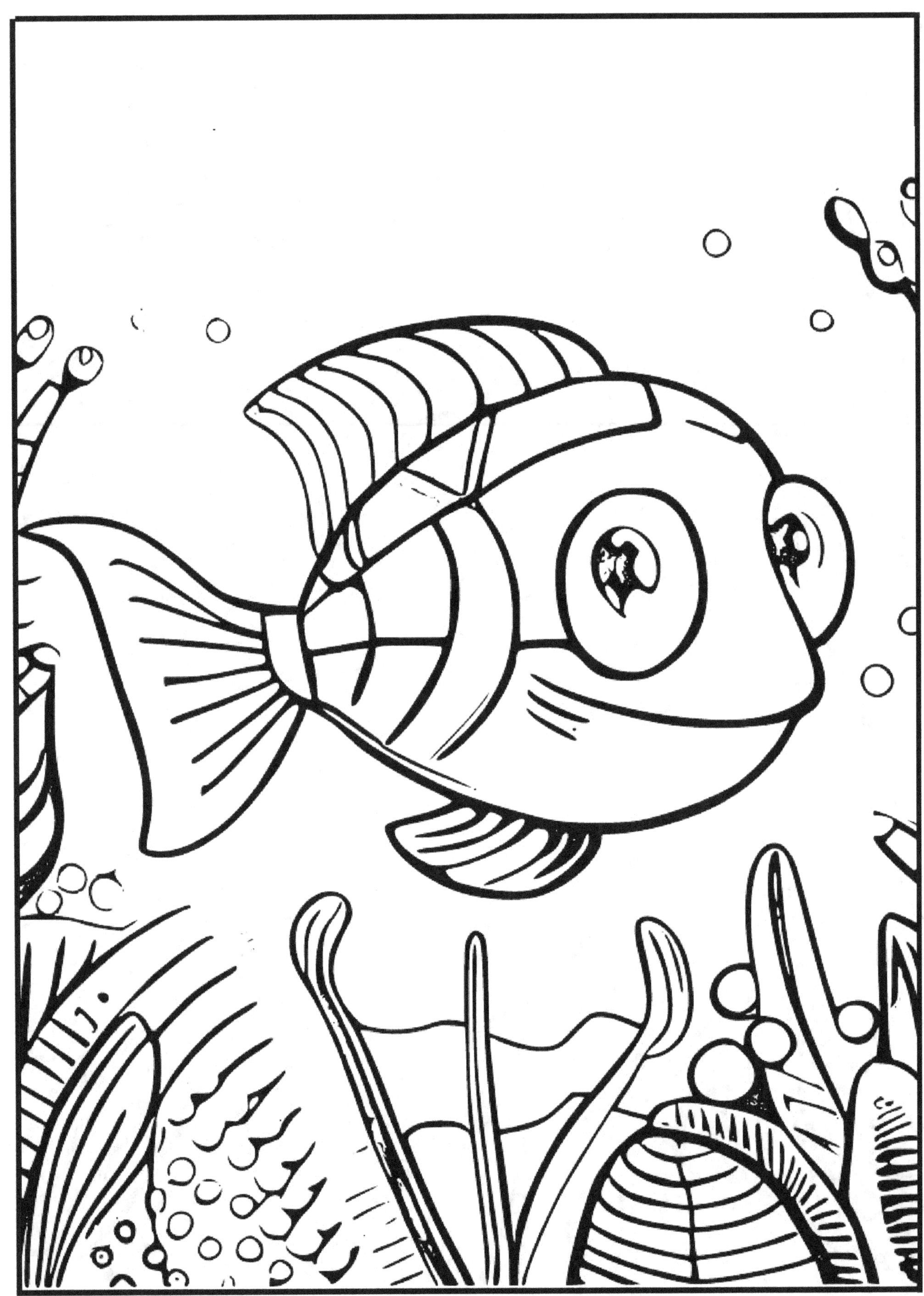

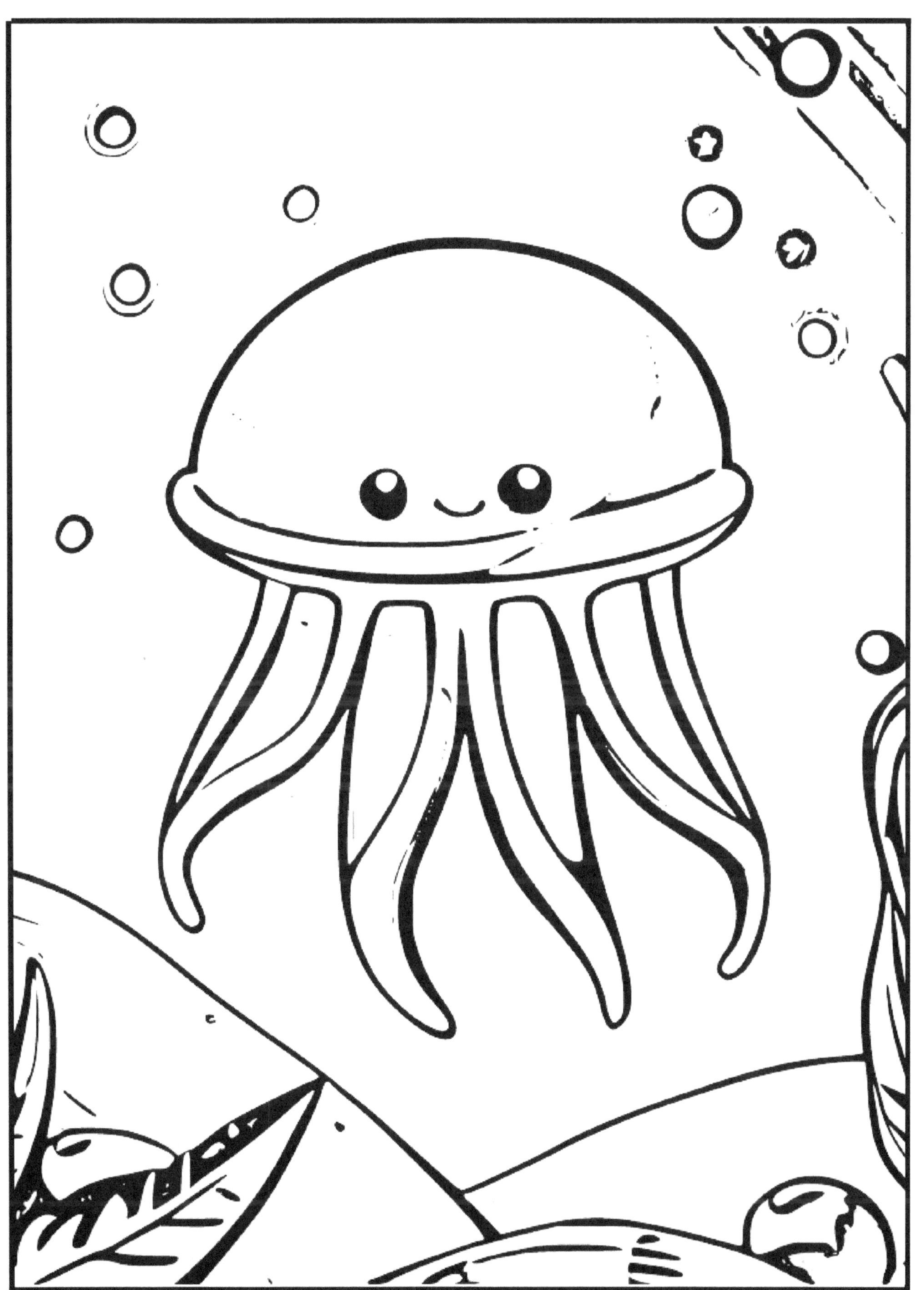

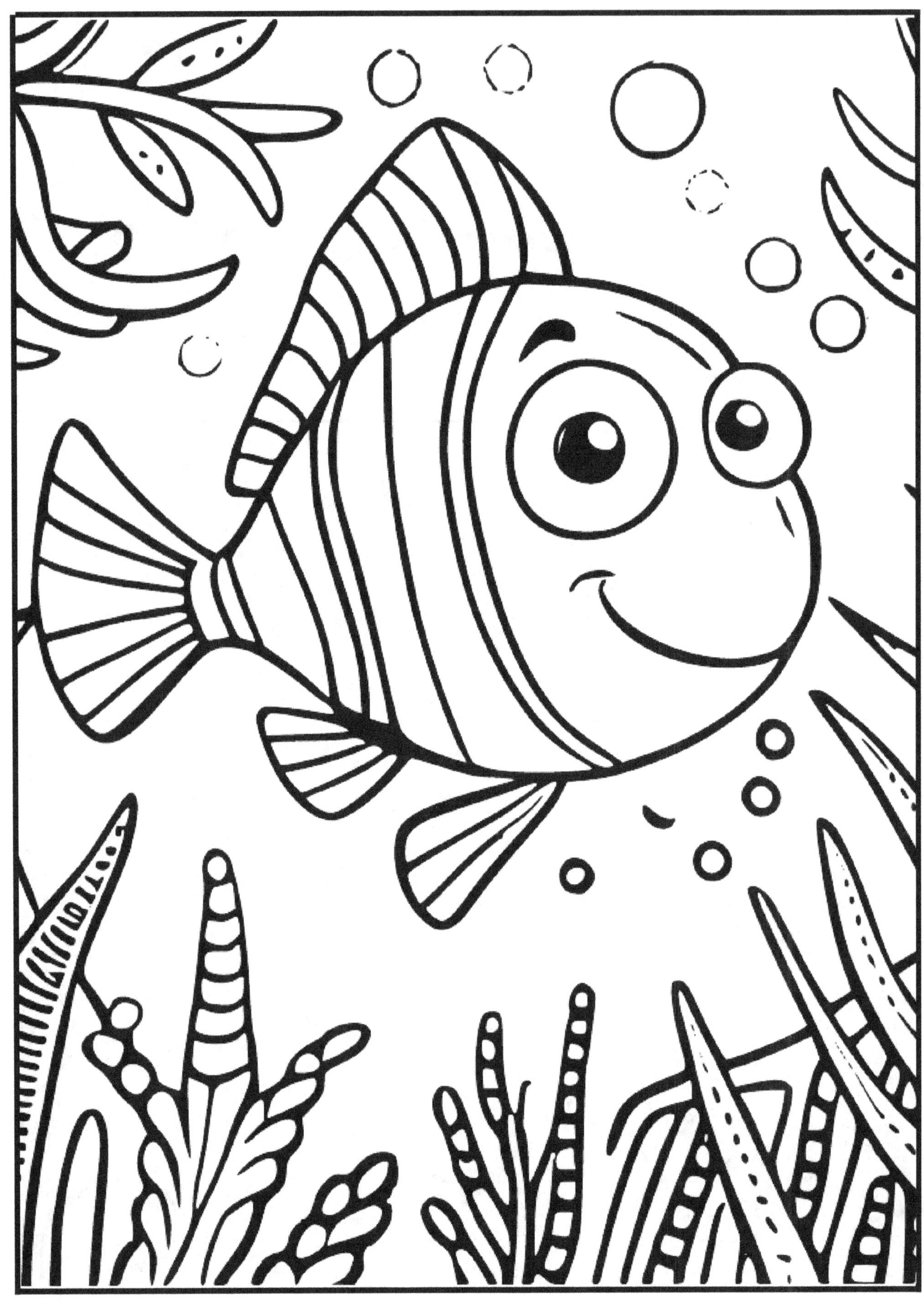

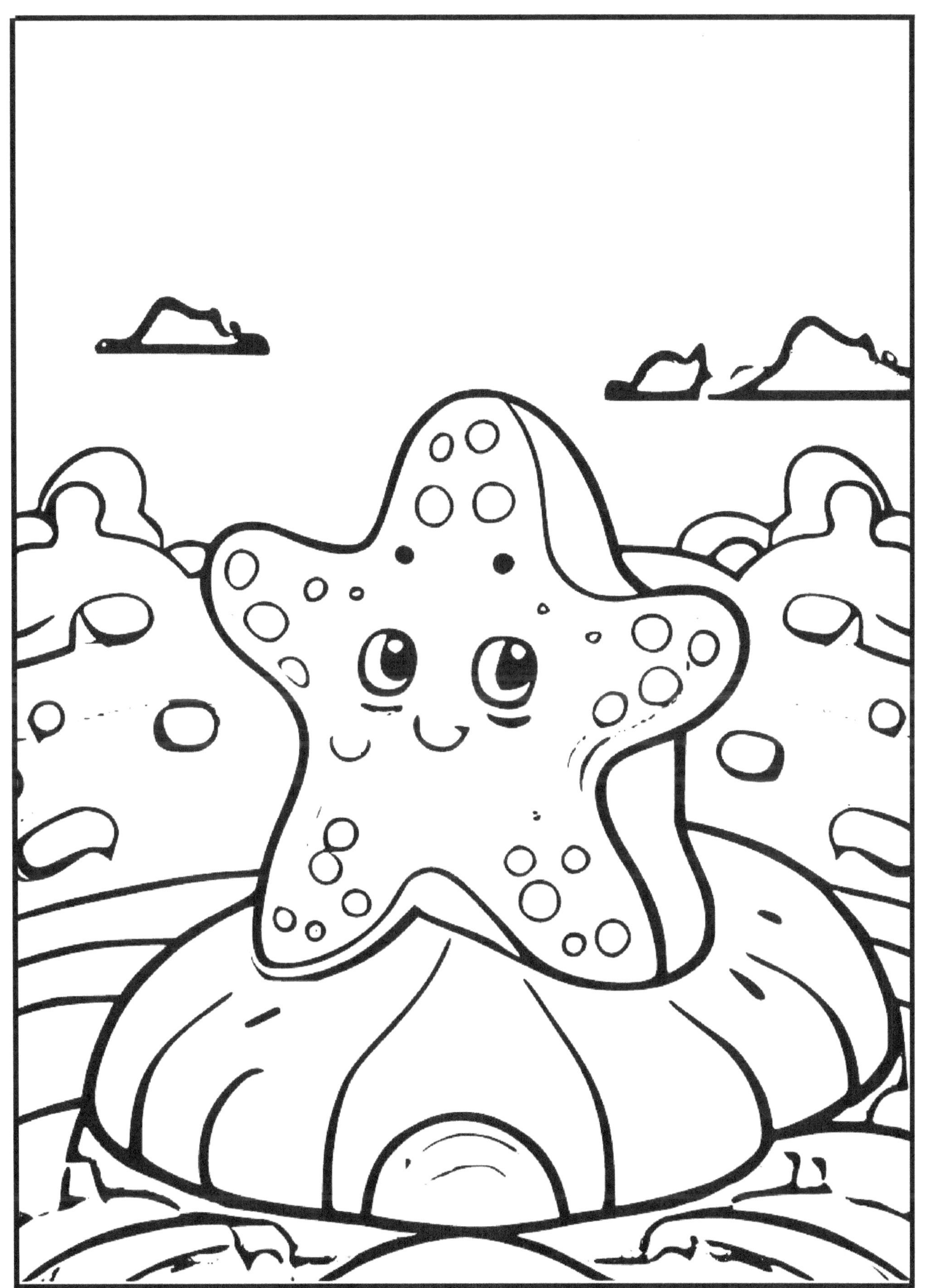

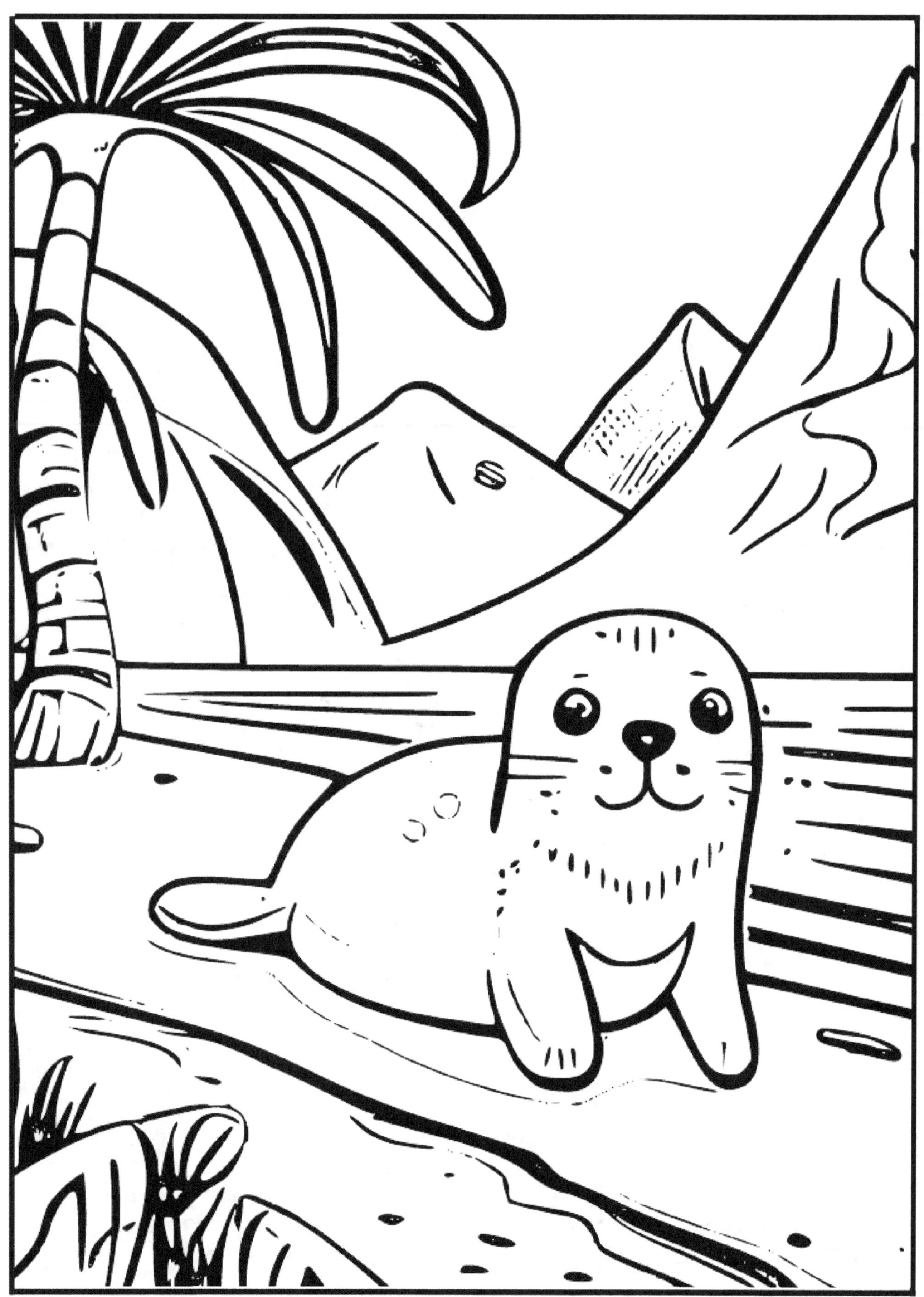

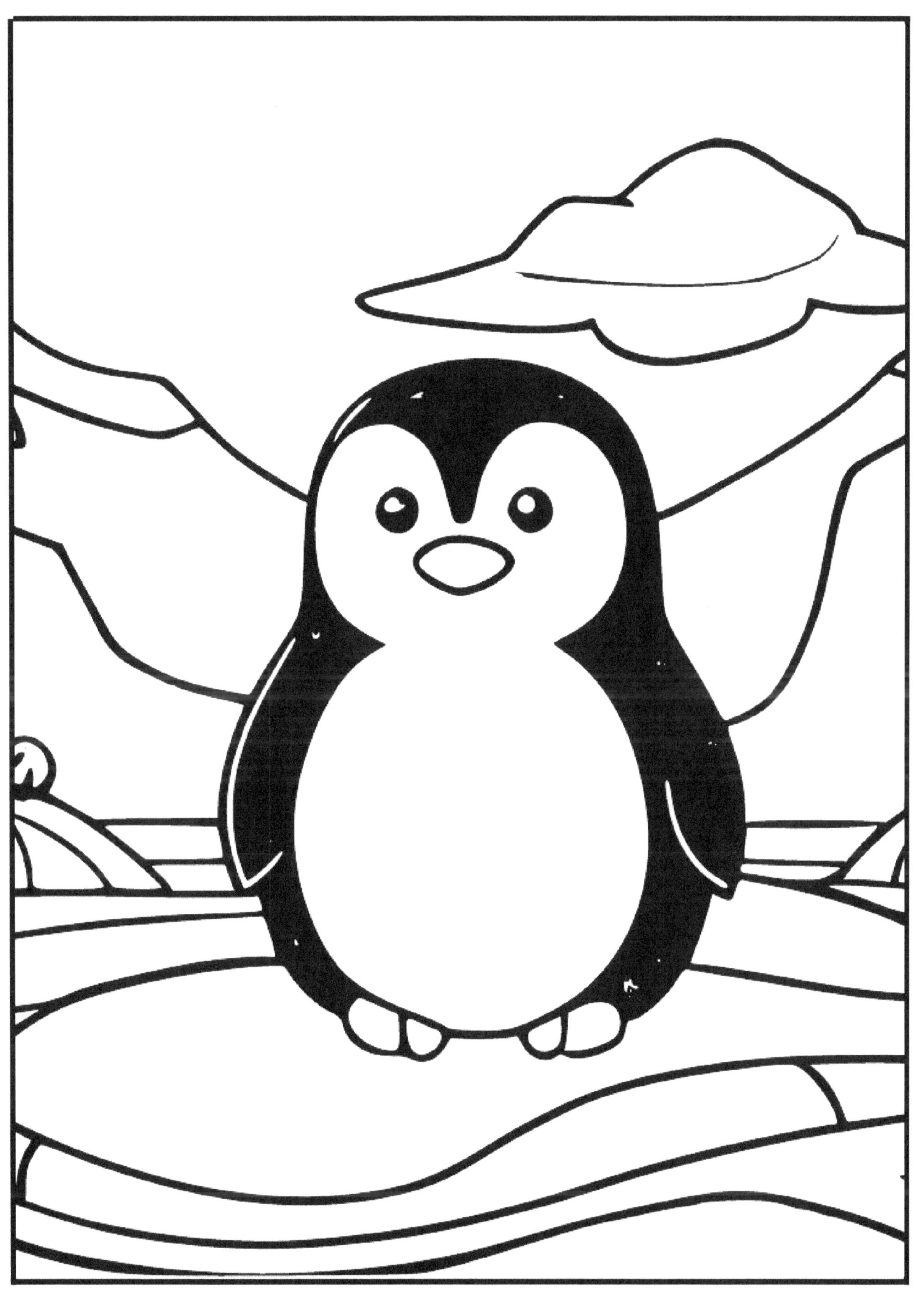

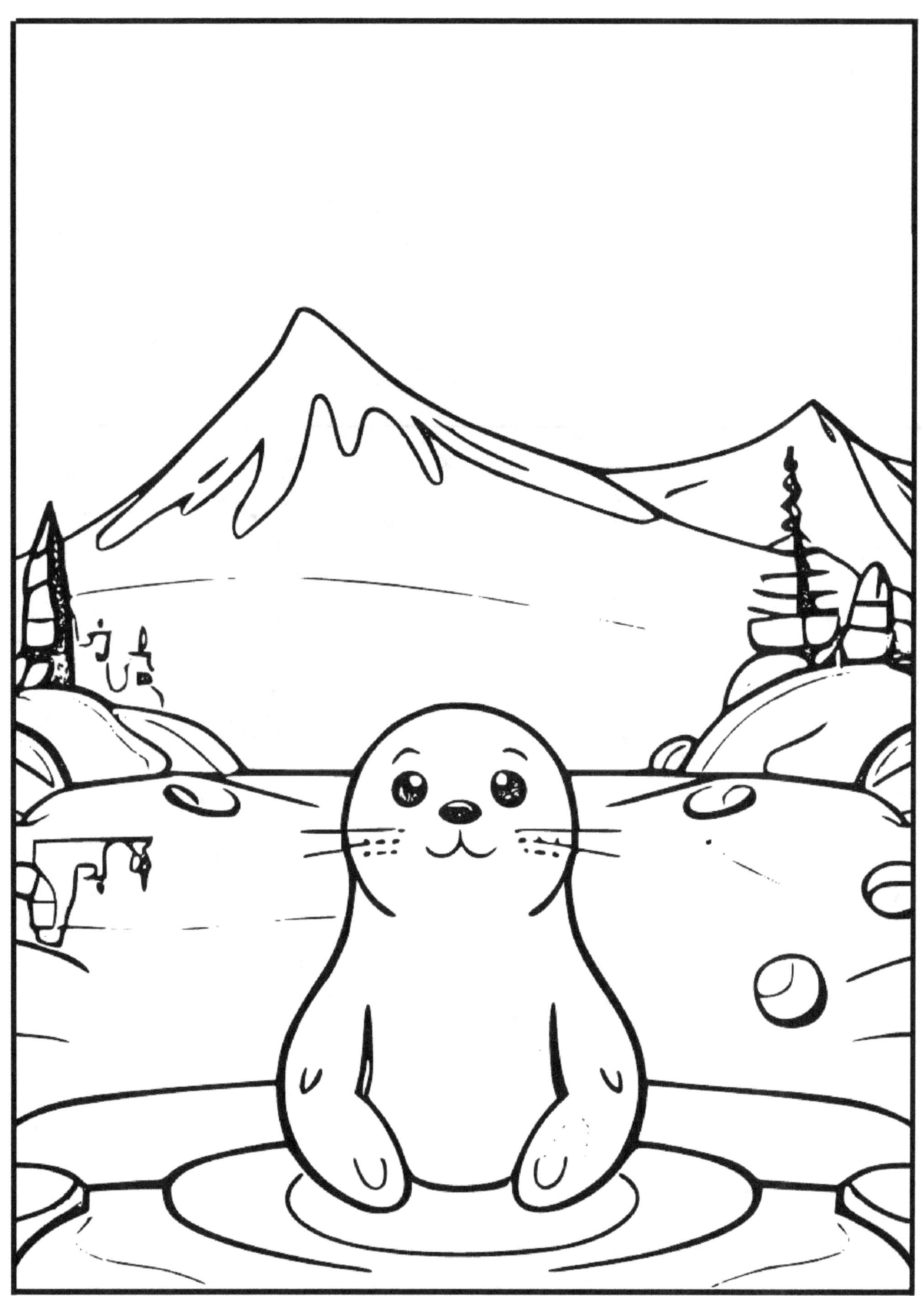

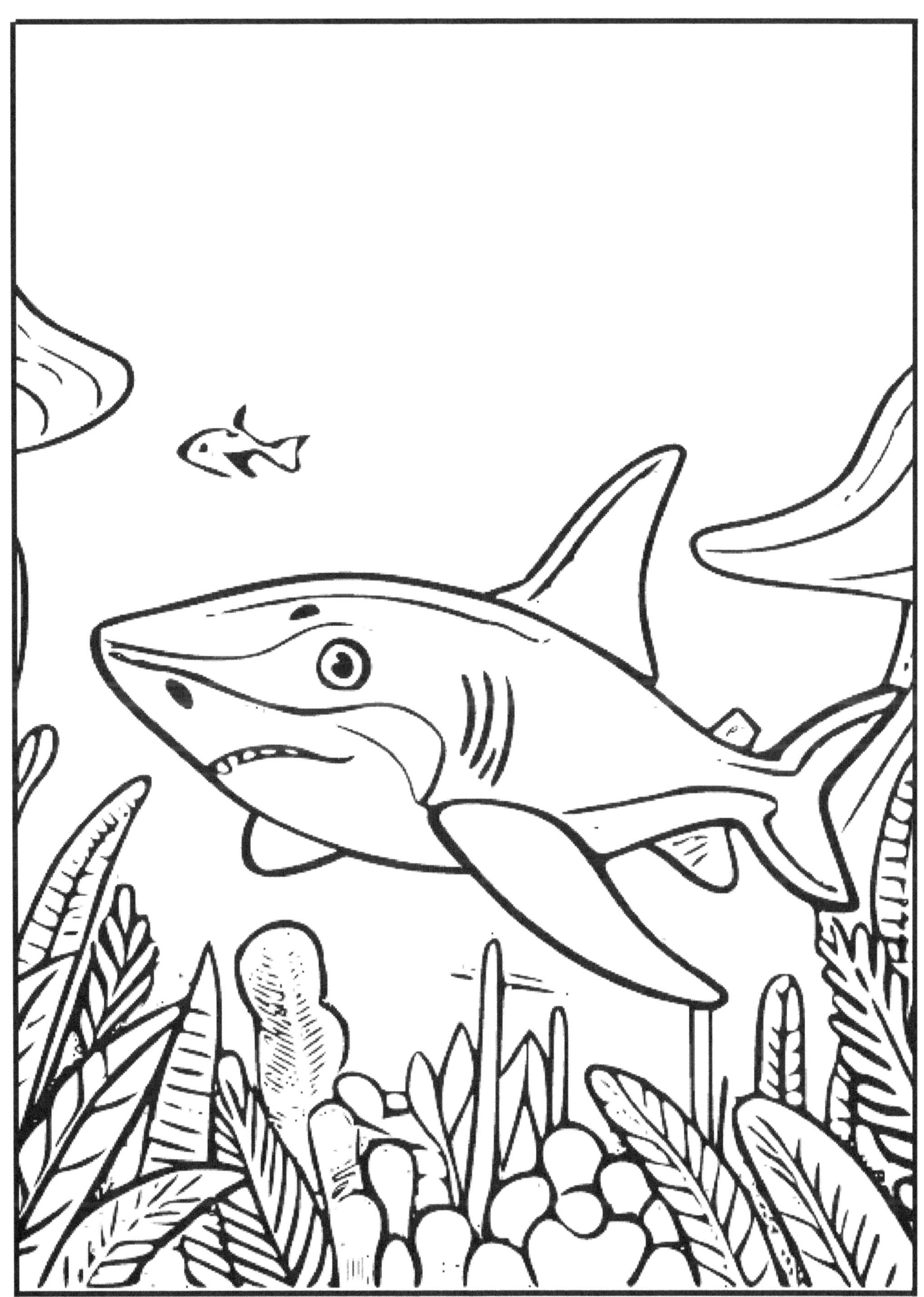

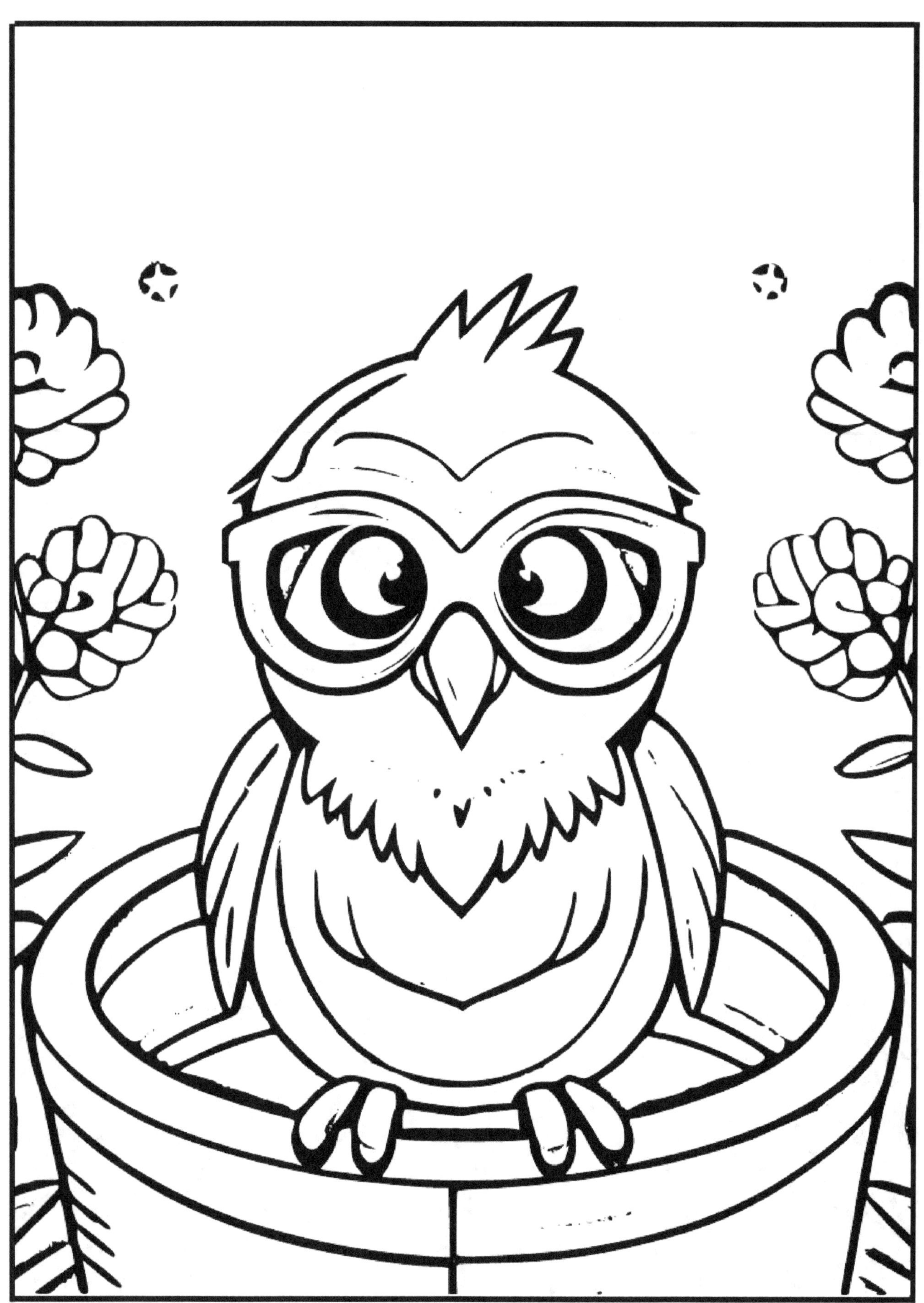

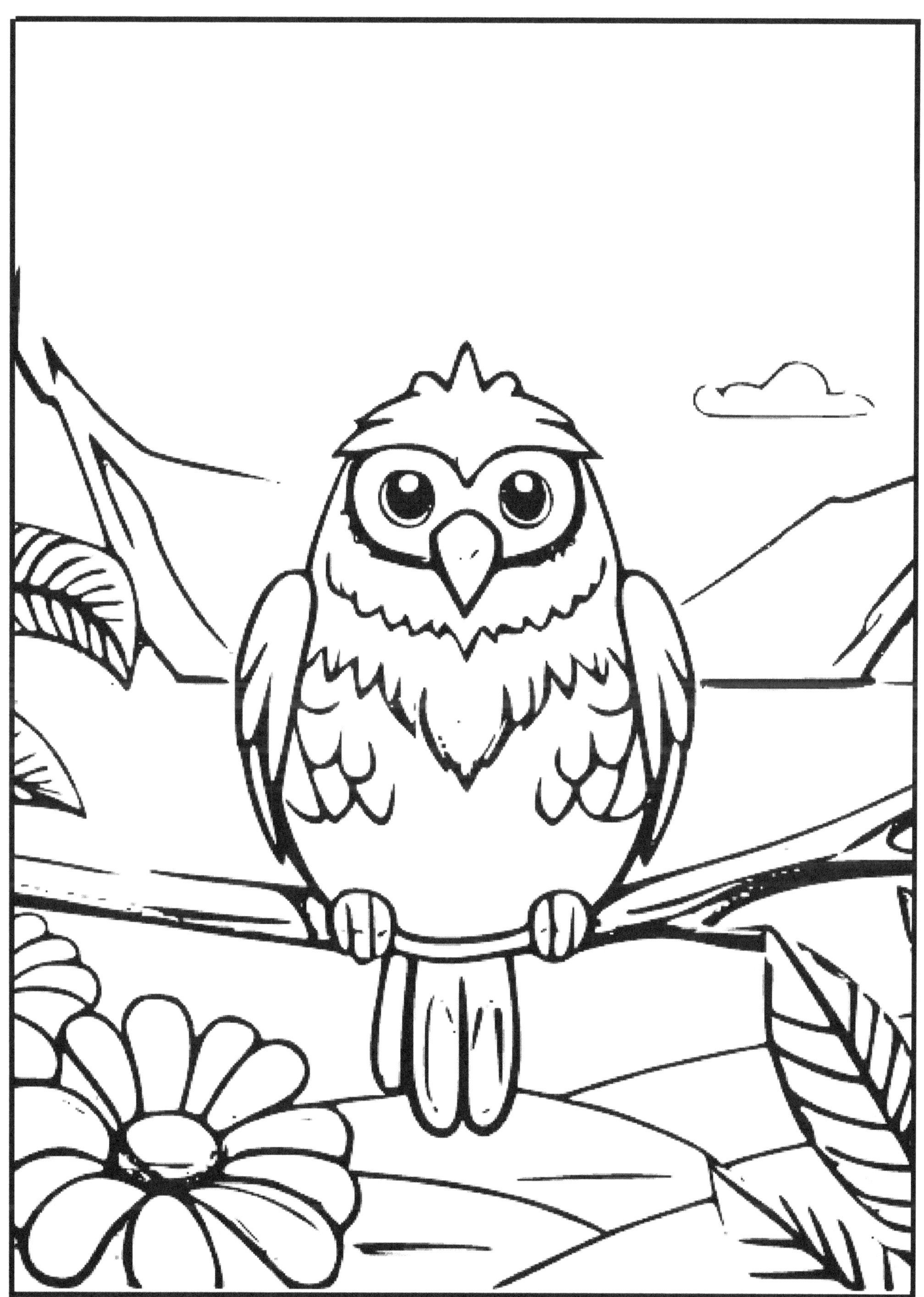

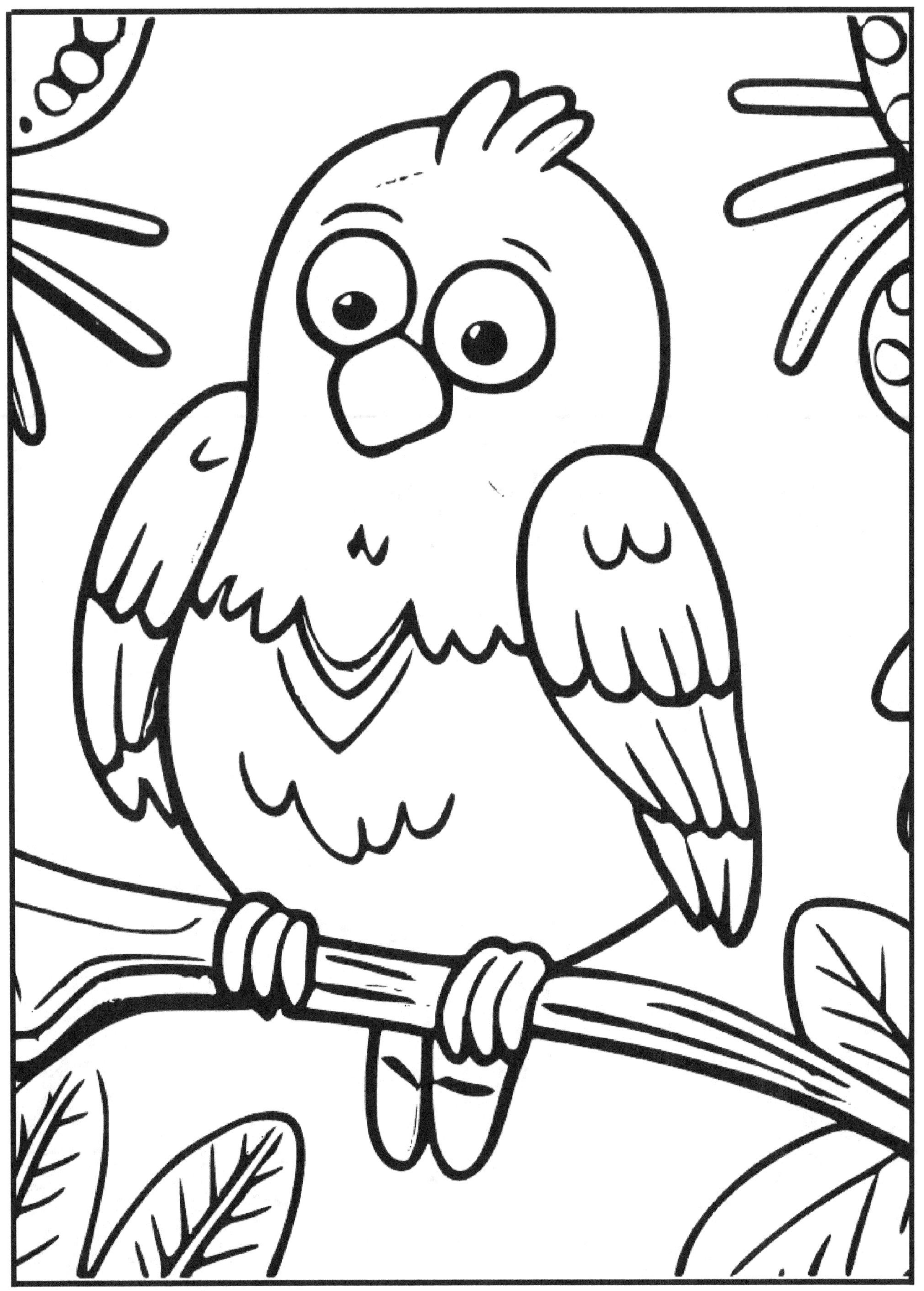

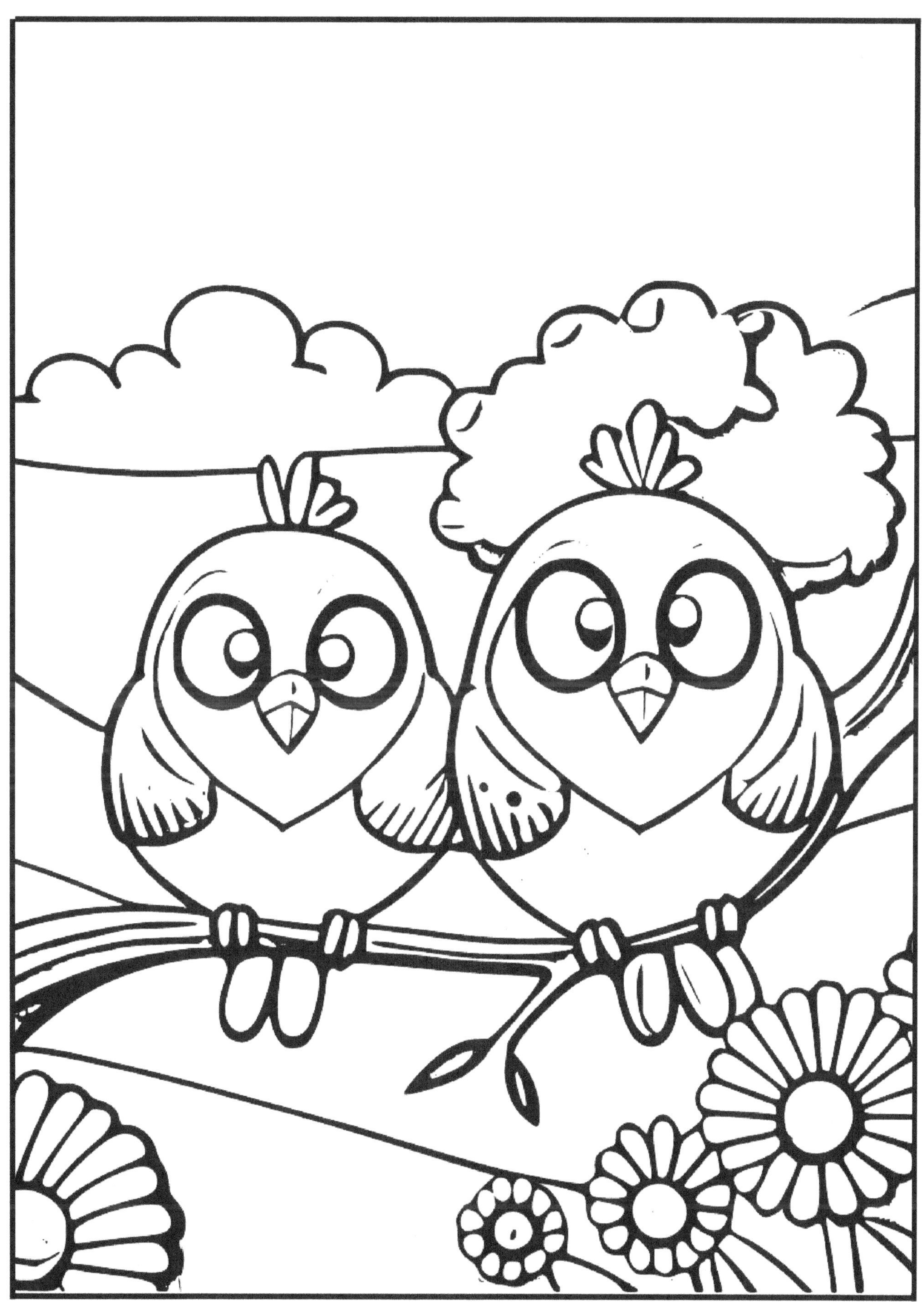

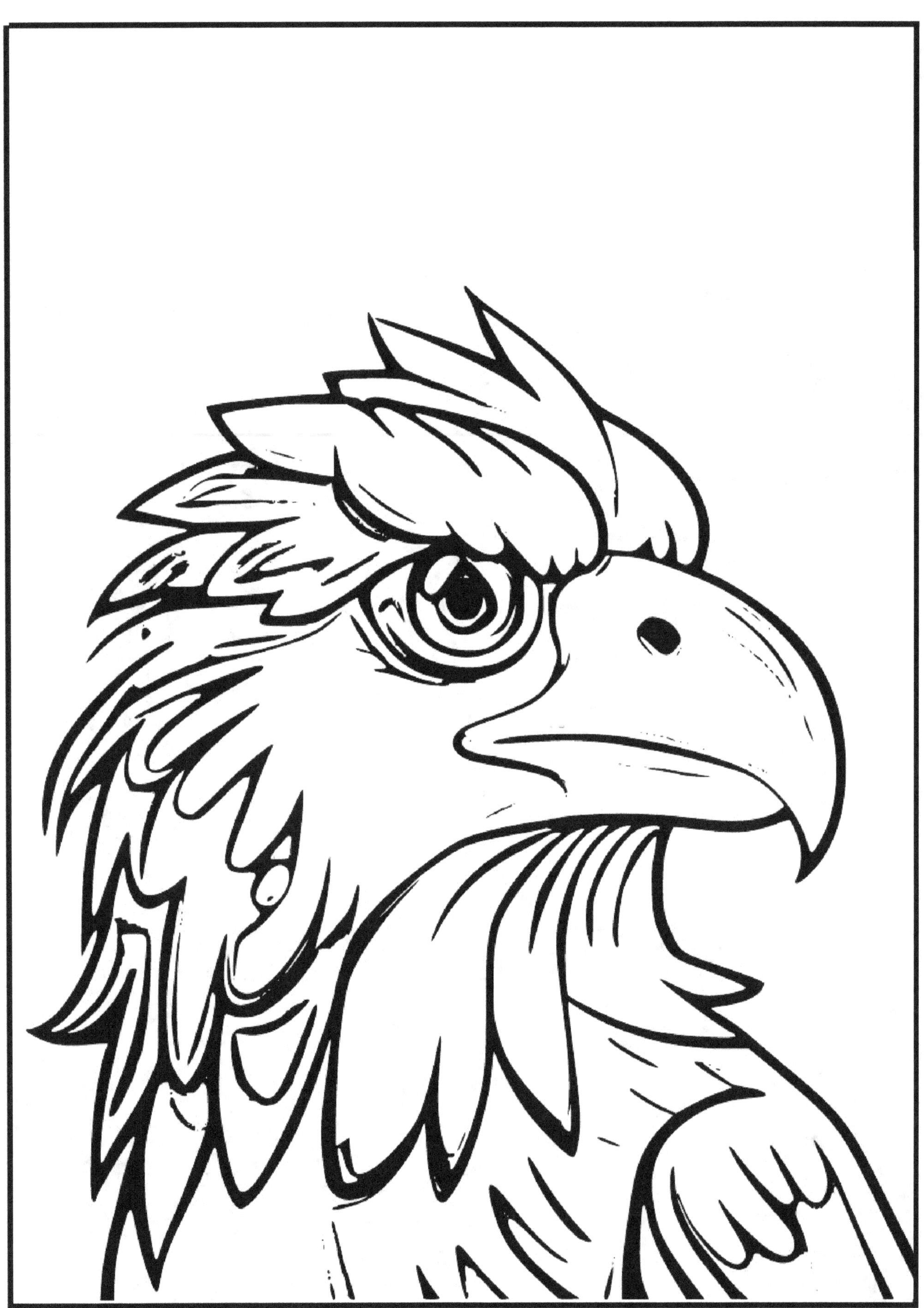

¡Que la magia del color y la imaginación los acompañe en cada trazo!